JOURNEY THROUGH
THE GRIEVING PROCESS
STEP BY STEP

Dr. Renee Sunday

© Sunday Publishing Company
Reneesunday.com
ISBN: 978-1-7334502-3-2

Table of Contents

Introduction

"Life is a process of accumulating losses. How we integrate or ignore, process or push away those losses -- of everything: jobs, friendships, relationships, health, things that matter to us -- starts to become patterns" - Donna Schuurman, family therapist, executive director emeritus, the Dougy Center, Portland, OR.

It's human nature to form deep connections with other people, animals, places, and things. The things you love provide you with an immense amount of joy and even give you a newfound purpose in your own life.

Yet, you can rarely fully prepare yourself for the loss of something near and dear to you. When such a traumatic loss occurs, both the body and mind respond in the form of grief.

The grieving process can be long and arduous, but it's absolutely necessary to move forward with your life.

Grief is very common. WebMD conducted a survey in 2019, "Grief: Beyond the 5 Stages," which surveyed 1,084 people and of those, 780 reported grieving a life event in the past 3 years, that's 72% of respondents.

In this guide, we'll go over the basics of what grief is, how grief typically manifests itself in humans, and how you can help guide yourself through the process and get to the other side.

"I grieve for all the losses, I grieve for all I lost, I grieve so I can walk through to the other side.
Anonymous

What Is Grief

According to the Mayo Clinic, grief is an intense period of sadness that typically follows some sort of loss or traumatic event. For the most part, grief is usually viewed as a period of mourning after something tragic occurs.

Grief is completely natural and is your mind's response to losing something you genuinely care about.

When grief becomes more severe, it can dramatically impact your ability to function physically, emotionally, mentally, and socially.

Types of Losses

Though we often link feelings of grief to a recent death, grief actually can occur with *any* type of loss that you might be dealing with. Here's a comprehensive list of other causes of grief.

- A recent and severe medical diagnosis or a worsening prognosis

- A loss of employment, a demotion, or an unwanted transfer

- A looming relocation where either you or somebody you care about is moving away

- An important relationship coming to an end, either romantic, familial, or platonic

- An end to an important chapter in your life, like a graduation or retirement

- A loss of a limb or a newly developed disability that causes limitations

- Grown children leaving the home (empty nest syndrome)

- Loss of identity

- Loss of a dream

- Loss of freedom, plans or even normal life as seen in the recent pandemic

Loss Hurts

- Changes in circumstances, for example, when you have to rework something in your life in order for something new to happen

- All types of changes can cause grief since when there is a change it means something is lost

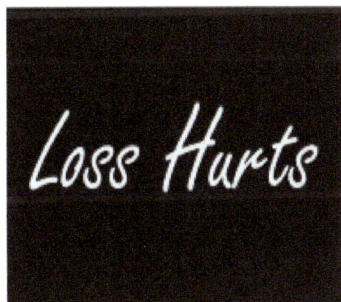

- And many others

What's unique about grief is that not all of these situations will cause a response in all people.

What causes you grief, in particular, depends on:

- Your personality
- Resilience
- Coping mechanisms
- Past losses
- How intensely you were attached to what you've lost

Different Types of Grief

Even though there's a clear definition of grief, that doesn't mean that everybody grieves in the same way. In fact, there are several different types of grief that impact if and how you deal with the loss after it actually occurs. Let's go over the other ways grief might show itself.

Abbreviated

Abbreviated grief is when you move on from a loss quicker than what's perceived as "normal." However, experiencing abbreviated grief doesn't necessarily mean that you simply didn't care about what you lost.

This type of grief sometimes occurs when you begin grieving *before* the actual loss happens (also known as anticipatory grief). This is common in situations where a family member is sick for a while and you begin to prepare yourself for the upcoming death.

Yet, it also might occur if you find a replacement for what you lost rather quickly. This could mean entering a new relationship after your spouse passes away or finding a new home after you lose yours to foreclosure.

Absent

Absent grief is simply grief that doesn't occur, or at least to the outside world. There are no outward signs of distress or emotions commonly associated with grieving an important loss, which means people might not even know that you're struggling.

This type of grief is sometimes seen in the caregiver role, where a person must put on a brave face and be strong for those around them. Other times, absent grief is simply a way to put your grief on hold until you can deal with it directly at another time.

Anticipatory

Anticipatory grief is the form of grief that occurs when you know a loss, or a death is coming. In a sense, you begin to prepare your body and mind for the loss so you're actually ready for it when it happens.

In some cases, you may have already imagined it in your mind and figured out how you would cope with it once it occurred. Even though you've come to terms with it sooner, anticipatory grief doesn't make the grieving process any easier or the loss any less traumatic.

Complicated

"About 7% of bereaved older adults, however, will develop the mental health condition of Complicated Grief (CG)" (Bereavement and Complicated Grief; M. Katherine Shearh et al, https://www.ncbi.nlm.nih.gov/pmc/articles/PMC3855369/#R2).

When grief continues well past the "normal" grieving period, it becomes complicated grief (or Persistent Complex Bereavement Disorder). Rather than being able to move past the loss, you find yourself unable to return to your normal everyday life.

With complicated grief, you're unable to let go of and accept the loss that you've experienced. When this type of grief becomes too severe, it can actually lead to the development of Major Depressive Disorder (MDD).

Collective

Collective grief is when an entire community or population is impacted by a loss and enters the period of mourning together. This type of grief is common in situations where many people are directly affected, including periods of war, natural disasters, and pandemics.

Cumulative

Cumulative grief is what occurs when you haven't properly dealt with another recent loss. This type of grief usually happens when several losses or traumatic events build-up one after another and seem to pile up uncontrollably.

Because of the massive amount of loss, cumulative grief has the potential to be the most intense type of grief there is. Rather than just dealing with just one loss, you now must deal with several, all at the same time.

Delayed

Delayed grief is grief that doesn't begin until well after a loss has occurred. It might be days, weeks, months, or even years before you formally acknowledge the loss and officially begin the grieving process.

What actually triggers the delayed grief is somewhat complicated. You might be reminded of what you lost (i.e. An image, voicemail, video, special location, or date) and then suddenly begin to grieve the loss.

Disenfranchised

Disenfranchised grief is grief that's typically hidden from the public eye. Usually, disenfranchised grief involves losses that you can't admit to the public or that others would view as "too much" or "too personal."

Some examples of disenfranchised grief include what's perceived as "minor" losses like the death or illness of a pet or a less serious boyfriend or girlfriend. Others include events that you chose to proceed with, including getting an abortion or filing for divorce.

Distorted

Not everyone grieves the same, and that's definitely the case with distorted grief. With this type of grief, your response to the loss is typically viewed as "unusual" and doesn't match up with what's considered to be "normal."

You might experience an intense period of hostility and self-destructive habits like substance abuse or self-harm. You also might begin to develop intense behavioral and personality changes that others around you are beginning to pick up on.

Exaggerated

Exaggerated grief produces quite serious mental health effects. In some cases, exaggerated grief can cause frightening nightmares, suicidal thoughts or ideation, self-harm, or even a substance abuse issue.

In more severe instances of exaggerated grief, a long-term mental health disorder might arise. For the most part, depression and anxiety are the most common and require immediate treatment by a medical professional.

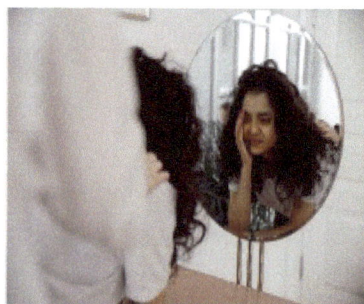

Inhibited

Inhibited grief is the type of grief that you typically keep to yourself, especially when you're around outsiders. When you experience inhibited grief, you might be extending the grieving process and limiting how much you're actually grieving.

Masked

Masked grief is characterized by physical symptoms that occur after you experience a loss. To be identified as masked grief, there have to be no other definitive triggers for what's causing your symptoms, which might be headaches, stomach aches, or other physical ailments.

The Importance Of Dealing With Grief

"You have within you, right now, everything you need to deal with whatever the world can throw at you. - Unknown

The better you deal with your grief, the more you're protecting yourself both mentally and emotionally. You'll be able to focus more on the positive aspects of your life rather than solely focusing your energy on your recent loss. Failing to address your grief as soon as possible will absolutely be detrimental to your wellbeing and healing process.

"Bereavement and its care are particularly relevant to older adults because they experience bereavement at a much higher rate than younger adults; one study found that over 70% of older adults experienced bereavement in a 2.5 year period" (Bereavement and Complicated Grief; M. Katherine Shearh et al, ttps://www.ncbi.nlm.nih.gov/pmc/articles/PMC3855369/#R2).

One way to look at the grief process is the journey of learning to accept the loss that has occurred and to find peace within yourself while living with that loss. This can be extremely difficult in some cases, for example the death of a loved one, especially a child or a spouse.

It can also be much easier for other losses, such as a breakup or a job loss. Though there are no set rules, for some even the later losses can be devastating, so it is very important to deal with any loss head on and go through a healthy healing process.

What Happens When We Deny Ourselves The Grieving Process

The pain and adversity you feel from a loss don't just go away. When ignored, grief and its effects will manifest in other ways, typically those which are not good for you.

You know that it's important to grieve because it allows you to move on, but it can also be extremely dangerous to avoid grieving altogether. Not only are you holding yourself back emotionally and mentally, but you're also putting yourself at serious risk for further issues.

Here's a look at what might occur when you deny yourself the grieving process.

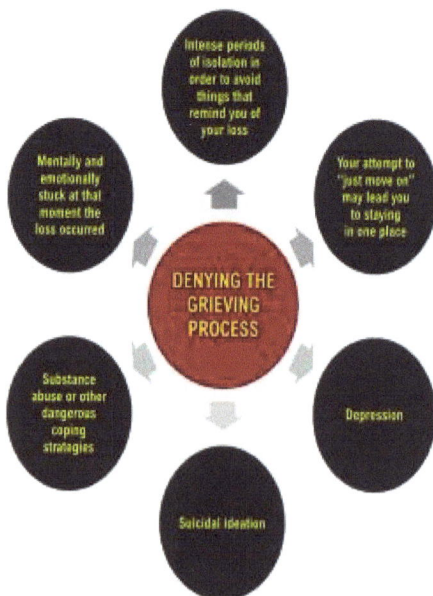

Intense periods of isolation in order to avoid things that remind you of your loss

Your attempt to "just move on" may lead you to staying in one place

DENYING THE GRIEVING PROCESS

Mentally and emotionally stuck at that moment the loss occurred

Substance abuse or other dangerous coping strategies

Depression

Suicidal Ideation

- Depression eventually develops and your mood will consistently remain low
- You might become suicidal and think about ending it all

- Intense periods of isolation in order to avoid things that remind you of your loss

- Substance abuse or other dangerous coping strategies in a desperate attempt to cope

- You're mentally and emotionally stuck at that moment the loss occurred

- Your attempt to "just move on" may lead you to staying in one place

Even though you might be uncomfortable showing your emotions, forcing yourself to skip the grieving process will only hurt you in the long run. It doesn't make you strong or invincible to pretend you aren't hurt and struggling.

How Others Respond

In WebMD's "Grief: Beyond the 5 Stages" survey, a whopping 53% of responders reported encounters with people whose "sympathy seemed to have an expiration date" (https://www.webmd.com/special-reports/grief-stages/20190711/the-grief-experience-survey-shows-its-complicated).

- 58% of those who lost a pet, a friendship or experienced a breakup said they felt people expected to see them recover within the first 3 months.
- 91% of those who were grieving a death related loss felt people expected them to move on within 1 year.

No one can know for sure why this happens, perhaps those people are uncomfortable with someone who is sad, sorrowful and grieving. Perhaps it scares them to see the manifestation of losses that can happen to them.

No matter their reasons, do not let this keep you from going through your own processes. There is no "externally set time limit to grieve," take the time you need, to feel and to process.

> "Keep your head up. God gives his hardest battles to his strongest soldiers. - unknown

Normal And Typical Grief Reactions

Even though everybody experiences and handles grief differently, medical experts have compiled a comprehensive list of several different emotional and physical symptoms that might occur in the grieving.

However, there's no guarantee that you'll experience any of these symptoms at all. In fact, a lot of it comes down to how well you handle grief, whether you have appropriate and healthy coping strategies, and how traumatic this loss was to you.

Emotional Symptoms Of Grief

88% of survey responders reported emotional symptoms while grieving (Grief: Beyond the 5 Stages"; WebMD; https://www.webmd.com/special-reports/grief-stages/20190711/the-grief-experience-survey-shows-its-complicated). 76% reported sadness and 43% said they experienced depression.

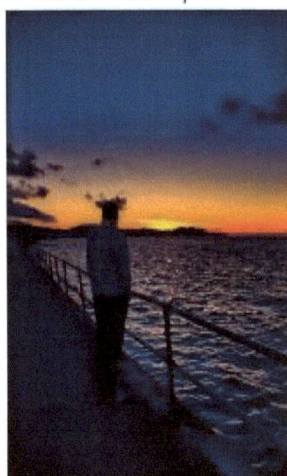

When you think of grief, you think of a profound wave or sense of sadness. With that said, here are some of the emotional symptoms of grief that are relatively common.

- Intense sadness or even depression

- Guilt and the sense that the loss was your fault

- Regret that you didn't do more to stop the loss from occurring

- Intense worry about the possibility of your own illness or death

- Lack of motivation to continue on with life

- Severe depression or anxiety

- Intense anger for no known reason

- Withdrawal and lack of desire to interact with others

- Lack of hygiene and desire to keep up with physical needs

If you already have a pre-existing mental health condition (like bipolar disorder, depression, or anxiety) or are still going through the grieving process from another recent loss, these emotional effects can be even more severe.

Physical Symptoms of Grief

68% of survey responders reported physical symptoms (Grief: Beyond the 5 Stages"; WebMD; https://www.webmd.com/special-reports/grief-stages/20190711/the-grief-experience-survey-shows-its-complicated). Of those fatigue was reported by 59% of survey responders and change of appetite by 48%.

What's unique about grief is that you might not even realize that the physical symptoms you're experiencing are your body's way of coping. Here are just some of the physical symptoms that have been linked to the grieving process.

- Low energy levels and extreme fatigue
- Inability to fall or stay asleep, or insomnia
- Weakened immune system and greater risk of the cold or flu
- Digestive issues like constipation, diarrhea, nausea, vomiting, or even acid reflux
- Tightness in the chest and breathing difficulties
- Headaches or other body aches with no known cause
- Weight gain or loss as a result of appetite changes

Broken Heart Syndrome

According to the American Heart Association, there's also a condition known as "Broken Heart Syndrome." This condition is also known as stress-induced cardiomyopathy, which is a severe chest pain that usually occurs after intense emotional stress or a recent traumatic loss.

> "Tough times never last, but tough people do.
> Robert H. Schuller

Grief Is A Healing Process: The Five Stages of Grief and Loss

"The reality is that you will grieve forever. You will not 'get over' the loss of a loved one; you will learn to live with it. You will heal and you will rebuild yourself around the loss you have suffered. You will be whole again but you will never be the same. Nor should you be the same nor would you want to."

In 1969, famed psychiatrist Elisabeth Kübler-Ross penned the now famous, On Death and Dying. In her book, she detailed what she refers to as the "five stages of grief and loss," which describe how humans typically respond to a traumatic death or loss.

Before we offer overviews of each of the five stages, keep a few things in mind. First, remember that not everybody experiences grief the same way, so what you experience could be totally different than another person going through the same exact type of loss.

You also might not go through all of the stages of grief f at all. It's very possible that you'll skip some stages and come back to them or just completely skip them without experiencing them at all during the grieving process.

Denial

The denial stage is the first stage of grief and is the typical first response to a major loss. During this stage, you might catch yourself saying things like, "This can't be happening," and maintaining a sense of disbelief.

You might begin wondering how you can even go on with your life if this loss really is occurring. Yet, there's also a possibility that you'll completely avoid the topic altogether, as if not formally acknowledging the loss means it actually isn't happening.

Anger

The anger stage is the first stage where you're actually demonstrating outward emotion. The anger you develop can be extremely intense, and you might find yourself snapping at or belittling those that you care most about.

For the most part, the anger stage is about finding somebody to blame or blowing off some steam. You want somebody to be responsible for the loss you're experiencing, whether it's the doctor that diagnosed your loved one, the person driving the other vehicle in an accident, the bank that took your home or even yourself or even yourself.

Though displayed as anger, this is truly just displaced pain. As the psyche tries to find a rationale for why the loss took place, in the initial stages, often there aren't not logical/acceptable answers. This lack of sense causes hurt which we experience and project as anger (Kubler Ross stages of grief. (n.d.). Retrieved from https://www.journey-through-grief.com/kubler-ross-stages-of-grief.html).

Bargaining

Even if you don't believe in God or a higher power, you might find yourself pleading with them for some extra time or attempt to negotiate some sort of deal. This stage is about being willing to do anything to reverse the loss and go back to normal life or have a little more time.

"what if" and "If only…" statements are extremely common in the bargaining stage. You might begin pondering whether there was something different that you or somebody else could've done to prevent the loss from happening in the first place.

Depression

The depression stage is where you really begin to feel the true emotion of the loss after you've finally acknowledged it mentally. You'll experience profound sadness and sorrow and find yourself thinking about the memories related to the person or thing that you've lost. You might become more withdrawn and lose motivation to engage with the outside world or keep up with hygiene. In this stage, it's not unusual for unhealthy coping mechanisms to develop, like self-harm, substance abuse, or reckless behavior.

Acceptance

Even though you come to terms with the loss during the acceptance stage, it doesn't mean that you're okay with it. It just means that you've acknowledged it happened, dealt with it, and are attempting to return to your normal life.

Yet, there really is no "normal" after such a traumatic loss that's impacted you emotionally and mentally. This is the stage where you'll attempt to rebuild your life around your loss, working to develop a "new normal."

"
What we have once enjoyed deeply we can never lose. All that we love deeply becomes a part of us.
Helen Keller

27 Ways To Find Comfort Through The Grieving Process: Taking Care Of Yourself

While you're attempting to get through the grieving process, the best thing you can do is learn to take care of yourself. Here are 27 of the best ways that you can help yourself through the process and get through to the other side.

1. **Deal with your feelings.** All the anger, sadness, sorrow, anguish, guilt, and other emotions that you are feeling must be dealt with. Talk to someone about them, write and journal, scream and beat on a pillow, just get them out.

2. **Talk to someone.** You might feel as if your emotions are becoming a massive burden to those around you, but that's completely false. It's in your best interest to find somebody that you can talk to who will listen to you talk without giving unsolicited advice.

3. **Take Things One Day At A Time.** You will have good days and bad days. Don't spend too much time worrying about when the grief is "over." Take each day one day at a time or even one minute at a time. Make sure to stay in the present moment, don't think about the past or future, just be in the here and now. This helps you from becoming overwhelmed and allows you to enjoy some moments of peace, which I promise will come.

4. **Write letters.** Whatever the loss you can write a letter or two to whatever or whomever you've lost. Say goodbye, tell it or him or her how you feel, how you will miss them, write them anything you want. You can write a letter to a friend who died but you can also write a letter to a lost dream, a lost job, anything really.

5. **Don't entirely avoid the subject.** Even though talking about the loss might upset you right now, not talking about it can prolong the grieving process. It's okay to say their name, look at old pictures, and think about them when you're feeling sad.

6. **Rid yourself of guilt.** You need to remind yourself that this loss had absolutely nothing to do with you. Holding onto any lingering guilt will destroy you mentally and emotionally and won't be conducive to moving on with your life.

7. **Make A Gratitude List.** Gratitude is healing. It heals you from within, promotes positivity and helps you to look at the bright side, which may be hard to find in times of great sorrow, sadness, and grief. Make a gratitude list and review it often. Focus on all that you have and all that you are.

8. **Lean On Your Faith.** In an article on Help Guide, psychologists Jeanne Segal, Ph.D. and Melinda Smith, M.A. say that faith is an incredible source of comfort following a loss. This applies to all types of losses in life, and not only those that are death related. A higher power can be found at churches and temples, but you can also find this source of faith in nature, around trees, lakes, rivers, creeks, and mountains.

9. **Don't put a time limit on your grief.** Some people believe that you should be completely over a loss in a year, but that's not true. Don't hold yourself to any standards regarding when you should be completely moved on, as everybody grieves differently.

10. **Reminisce.** Spend some time thinking about the positive memories you experienced with your deceased loved one. Focus more on the joy you had spending time with them, places you've been together, and things you liked to do that made you both happy.

11. **Consider grief therapy.** By finding a licensed grief counselor, you can better cope with the grieving process and develop more positive coping strategies. You'll learn new ways to deal with your emotions and how to move past the loss in due time.

12. **Pamper yourself.** You've dealt with a lot in the last few weeks and months, so it's time to do something just for you. Maybe go to the spa and sit in

the sauna, get your nails done, get a relaxing massage, or try out a new haircut.

13. **Remember to eat.** Your appetite will be totally off-balance when you're grieving and it's very normal to have very little appetite and lose weight. Try your best to eat several times per day, even if you're only eating a little bit of food during each meal.

14. **Avoid substances.** You know how calming it might be at first to smoke a cigarette, drink some alcohol, or try other drugs. Yet, substances are very addictive and might only intensify the emotions associated with grief, so do your best to avoid them.

15. **Think about group therapy.** Not everybody likes sharing their emotions with strangers, but group therapy is a great way to deal with your grief. In a grief group, you can share your story, learn about how others are coping, and even make some lifelong friends.

16. **Remember that you're not alone.** Even though you're isolating yourself and withdrawn socially, it doesn't mean that you're alone. There are likely other people that are dealing with the same loss and it's okay to lean on one another when the emotions get tough.

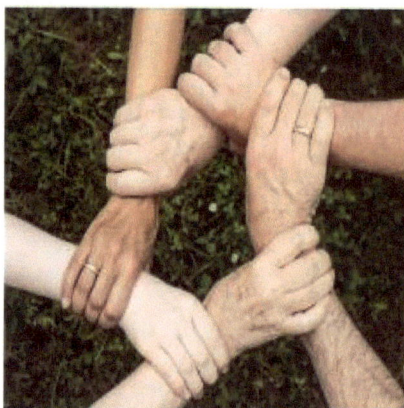

17. **Honor the legacy of your loved one.** One of the best ways to cope with your grief is by honoring your loved one. You might think about decorating a room the way they would've wanted, planting a tree in their honor, or even purchasing a nice memorial plaque.

18. **Do something you enjoy.** When you're grieving a loss, you might feel guilty about smiling, laughing, or experiencing happiness. It's okay and actually recommended that you put yourself first and do something you find fun and enjoyable instead of grieving.

19. **Explore the world.** Getting out of the house is the best thing you can do when you're alone and grieving. Try going to your local park, trying out some of the easy hiking trails, going to a nature preserve, or just going on long drives down peaceful country roads.

20. **Give back.** In honor of your loved one, you can think about giving back to those who really need it in your community. This might mean donating blood to the local hospital, spending some time at the local food pantry, or volunteering at an animal shelter.

21. **Listen To Soothing Music.** Music is incredibly powerful in how it affects the brain. It can induce a wide range of feelings, including calm, peace, and serenity and even happiness. Create a playlist that calms you and brings you comfort in your time of grief.

22. **Do something positive with your grief.** When you're overwhelmed with sadness, it's useful to turn your sadness into something positive. You can do this by picking up a new hobby, trying to make new friends, or making a gratitude list on what you're thankful for.

23. **Don't isolate.** The worst thing you can do is distance yourself from people. Do your best to keep up with your relationships and reach out to people you care about. They want to hear from you, but they might not be sure how to start the conversation right now.

24. **Show your love.** When you experience a loss, it's quite common to feel as if life is short and can be taken from you at any moment. So, make it a point to remind the most important people in your life that you care about and highly value them.

25. **Find an emotional support animal.** Emotional support animals are actually really great for keeping you from getting lonely and supporting you during the tougher moments of grief. Plus, you can adopt a cute cat, dog, rabbit, and nearly any other animal.

26. **Look to the bright side.** In regard to losses other than death, consider the bright side. Whenever a door closes another opens. What opportunities or gifts have you received as a result of this loss? For example, perhaps you have lost a job, consider that this loss will make you stronger, more resilient, a better problem solver and someone who will overcome a major challenge, aren't all of these things a bright side? A very bright side?

27. **Remember that the bad times won't last forever.** Right now, your grief seems endless and is often unrelenting. Yet, you've overcome everything in your life up until this point. Stick to that mindset and remember that things will get better eventually.

Not all of these things will work for everybody, so try to pick items from the list that seem reasonable in *your* life.

The goal here is to allow yourself the proper amount of time to grieve, but also continue on with your life as much as possible and to avoid drowning in pain and sorrow.

> "How lucky I am to have something that makes saying goodbye so hard."
> Winnie the Pooh

Grief: 6 Myths And Facts

Grief is a highly misunderstood topic. There's a common belief that everybody

handles grief the same and everybody goes through the five stages of grief as usual, but there's actually a lot more to grief than what meets the eye.

We want to dispel any myths that are still circulating about grief and hit you with some hard-hitting facts to help you through the grieving process.

Myth #1: Grief only occurs after death

Grief is most commonly associated with a recent death, but that's not always the case. You might experience grief when you go through any type of loss, whether you've lost your job, suddenly became disabled, ended a relationship, or received a poor medical diagnosis.

Yet, there's no guarantee that you'll even experience grief after death at all. When your grief manifests in the form of absent grief, you might show no outward signs of emotion or distress, even if the death was of somebody very close to you.

Myth #2: Everybody goes through the five stages of grief

When Elisabeth Kübler-Ross wrote On Death and Dying, her theory involved a typical response to grief and loss. Though most people experience some type of grief after a loss, there's really no guarantee that grief will even occur.

It's highly possible that you'll skip one of the stages and eventually revert back to it later in the grieving process. It's also not unusual to completely miss a stage and come out on the other side without ever going through all five stages.

Myth #3: There's a set timeframe for getting over a loss

Some people think that you should be completely over death within a year's time, but there should never be a timeline when it comes to grief. Some people struggle a lot more than others and grieving the loss of a person very close to you can be mentally and emotionally taxing.

If you hold yourself to this one-year timeframe, you might only be setting yourself back even further. You might force yourself to accelerate the process or skip some stages of grief, which might only extend the process or cause it to rear its ugly head at a later date.

Myth #4: You just have to get over it

This one is much easier said than done. If everybody were able to simply "get over it" with a snap of their fingers, don't you think they would've done that by now instead of letting the sadness destroy them mentally, emotionally, and physically?

The grieving process is important to go through at your own rate. Plus, you need to spend more of your time focusing on getting *through* the trauma of the loss, not simply getting *over* it as if it's that easy to leave behind you.

Myth #5: If you're not crying, you just don't care.

There should never be any standards for what's considered "normal" when it comes to how you grieve. Just because you're not crying or an emotional wreck while you're out in public doesn't mean the loss really didn't impact you.

Some people just grieve differently. Some would rather express themselves on their own time when they're alone while others might let their grief out through other outlets like their passions and their hobbies.

Myth #6: Grief comes to an end

The truth is it does not really end, but it does change over time. The process of grief and all the personal emotions and dynamics that go with it is an ever-changing process, it can change minute by minute and year by year. Various triggers, such as memories, a scent, a photo or even a word can bring the intensity of grief back to the forefront at any time, even years after having suffered that loss.

> "
> And once the storm is over, you won't remember how you made it through, how you managed to survive. You won't even be sure whether the storm is really over. But one thing is certain. When you come out of the storm, you won't be the same person who walked in. That's what this storm's all about.
> Haruki Murakami

When To Seek Professional Help

Talking with a mental health professional may be helpful in any case, as a therapist can be a great source of comfort and healing.

If you've never experienced an intense amount of grief before, it might be difficult to figure out when you should seek professional help. After all, you might feel like you're handling it pretty well on your own right now.

Sometimes, it becomes absolutely necessary to seek professional help.

Here are some signs it's time to get help.

- The most common reason that people get professional help for their grief is that it's lasting longer than usual. Your entire life is suddenly centered around the loss and you can't do anything without being brought down by these negative thoughts.

- Your appetite is practically non-existent, and you have to force yourself to even eat a small bit of food.
- Sleeping is nearly impossible even though you're extremely tired and have been awake for what seems like days now.
- You might experience panic attacks for no reason at all.
- You've lost your desire to take showers, clean up the house, or care for your children or pets.

- The most definitive sign that you need professional help is if you're experiencing any form of suicidal thoughts.

Grieving is hard, but you don't have to do it alone and there are plenty of people and organizations out there that are willing to support you.

Getting Help And Support

At a certain point, it's just not reasonable to expect to be able to handle your grief alone. If you've noticed any of the reasons we went over in the previous section in your own life, it's time to reach out and put yourself first.

You can do so in a variety of ways, either leaning on those closest to you or seeking more intensive, professional help.

Finding Emotional Support In Your Inner Circle

The first thing that most people do is find somebody that they can trust. This can be a family member, a friend, a coworker, a boss, or a teacher that you feel particularly close to.

The best quality to look for in your support figure is someone that's a good listener. You want somebody that'll listen to you as you open up about your feelings, not somebody who's going to interrupt you and give you unsolicited advice.

If your go-to support system is also struggling with the loss, it might be helpful to lean on each other. Yet, this can also be counter-productive, so you should also have somebody to turn to that's not involved.

A lot of people who are grieving are wary of turning to those who need help. Just remember that everybody needs support and, one day, they just might need to lean on you too.

Organizations

If you're having trouble finding somebody you can lean on, there are plenty of organizations out there that'll connect you to a support group or a therapist that can help you out. Here are a few examples of grief organizations you might want to look into.

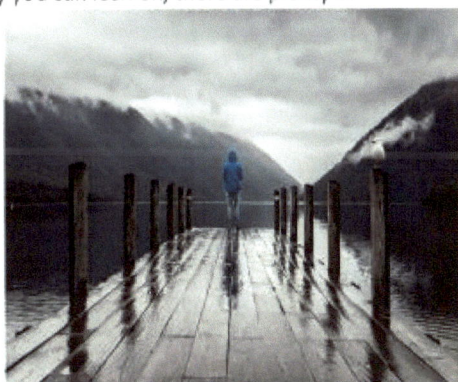

- The Compassionate Friends. This is one of the most widespread grief organizations in America, having representation in all 50 states, Washington D.C., Puerto Rico, and Guam. The group focuses on providing support for those grieving a recent death.

- National Alliance for Grieving Children. This organization is specifically for children and teenagers grieving a death. The organization focuses on providing education and support to children who are struggling.

- Bereaved Parents USA. This organization was built for parents struggling with the recent loss of a child. The organization works to connect you to other families who are also struggling where you can then encourage one another.

- Actively Moving Forward. This organization is for young adults and college-aged people. The focus of the group is to find support through your loved one's memory.

Many grief organizations are also great resources for learning about the coping and grieving process and how you can work to move on peacefully. Some even offer events where you can get together with other grieving families and do something enjoyable.

Therapeutic Means

When it's time to get professional help, there are two major avenues you can consider taking: Individual grief therapy and grief groups. Let's go over what each is and the potential benefits of each of them.

Most people prefer *individual grief therapy*. Find a licensed therapist that specializes in grief and coping with losses for the best experience. While there, you can talk about the loss and come up with coping strategies to make the grieving process just a little bit easier.

According to the Hospice Foundation of America, *grief groups* are great for validating your loss and building empathy toward others that are struggling. At group meetings, you can share your story, lean on one another for support, and figure out how to cope with the loss.

One study found that when grief is treated with trauma-based therapy, it yielded a 25% better response rate than traditional forms of therapy (Treatment of Complicated Grief, A Randomized Controlled Trial, M. Katherine Shearh et al, https://jamanetwork.com/journals/jama/fullarticle/200995).

Losses Other Than Death

Non-death related losses in life can be devastating. Don't be afraid to seek professional help in those cases. Loss of dreams, identity, empty nest syndrome and other losses can be dealt with, you can recover and grow as a person while building resilience and inner strength AND you don't have to do it alone.

At the end of the day, you need to do what's best for you. Find the method that fits into your lifestyle and try something new if what you're already doing isn't working too well.

> "Everybody goes through difficult times, but it is those who push through those difficult times who will eventually become successful in life. Don't give up, because this too shall pass."
> Jeanette Coron

Grief Vs. Depression: What's The Difference?

There's a very fine line between grief and depression and, sometimes, they're difficult to differentiate between. Let's go over some of the major similarities and differences between grief and depression, according to the Dana Foundation for brain research.

With both conditions, you might experience ruminating thoughts, particularly about the loss of your loved one or negative thoughts about yourself. You'll feel a persistent low mood and might lose motivation to do the things you once loved.

Generally, you just aren't happy like you used to be. You might not have an appetite at all and begin to lose a significant amount of weight. Even though you're extremely tired and weak, insomnia is really common, and you might lie awake at night just thinking about the bad things.

The major difference between the two is that grief usually comes in waves while depression is rather consistent. Yet, persistent grief can eventually turn into depression if left untreated.

When Grief Becomes Depression

This typically results from most types of complicated grief, also known as the grief, that doesn't seem to be going away any time soon. It's like you're stuck in your grief and can't move past it like you normally would.

So, how do you know when grief has become depression? It mostly comes down to the intensity of the grief. If the grief that used to come in waves is suddenly there day in and day out, you might be facing depression.

When your grief doesn't appear to be slowing down, it might be time to consider getting outside help. Individual grief therapy and grief groups are a great first step at healing yourself when you realize that your grief may have become depression

"
Cherish what you can control, let go of that which you cannot.
Anonymous

Pandemic Related Grief And Loss

As we've already mentioned, grief isn't only about death. In fact, you can grieve nearly anything that's been taken from you.

That's why grief is very common in a pandemic, even if you haven't been personally affected by the virus or disease. There are plenty of other losses that occur during such trying times that often go unnoticed.

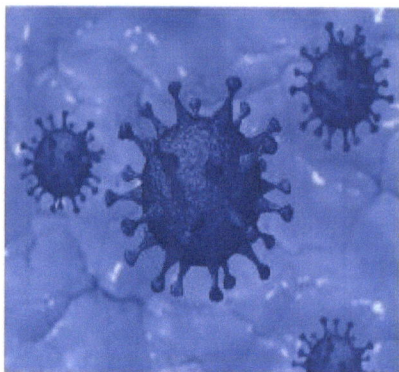

Other Types of Losses

Think about what life is like while living in a pandemic. You're trapped at home, only allowed to leave the home at certain hours of the day for emergencies or to buy essential goods like groceries or gasoline.

Work and school have essentially been canceled indefinitely. Nearly every plan that was scheduled for the near future is on hold until the pandemic finally breaks, and the world goes back to normal.

Here are some other types of losses common in a pandemic.

- **Loss of freedom.** You're mourning the loss of being able to do what you once did without a second thought. You can't go to the park to go for a jog, go to the grocery store when it's convenient for you, or even hang out with your friends at the restaurant.

- **Loss of people.** You're no longer allowed to socialize with people you really care about. Your interactions are limited to simple phone calls, text messages, and video chats, but it never seems like enough and is definitely nothing like it used to be.

- **Loss of control.** You're no longer in control of your own life. You're forced to stay home from work or school, the government is deciding where you're allowed to go and when, and there's nothing you can do about it for the near future.

- **Grief for the suffering.** People are being diagnosed with a fatal illness and some are losing their lives. Experiencing grief for the people who are suffering demonstrates empathy and that you genuinely care about other people.

- **Loss of work.** It's not just about having somewhere to go every morning. You now don't have a steady paycheck to bring home to your family and you're finding it difficult to pay the mortgage or keep food on the table. According to Aff.org, *"Research shows that job loss is associated with increased depression, anxiety, distress, and low self-esteem and may lead to higher rates of substance use disorder and suicide. Recent polling data shows that more than half of the people who lost income or employment reported negative mental health impacts from worry or stress over coronavirus."*

- **Loss of the world as we know it.** Things aren't the same right now, and you have no idea when they will be back to the way they once were. Right now, you're struggling with the thought that things will be permanently changed.

- **Loss of plans.** Everybody had plans for the next few weeks and months. Graduations, parties, weddings, family vacations, and even funerals have been put on hold for the time being, with nobody knowing if and when they'll be allowed to happen in the future.

You might feel guilty feeling grief during the pandemic if you or someone you know hasn't been diagnosed with the illness. Yet, that doesn't mean that your grief isn't justified or that you're selfish in any way.

> **"**
> It is only in our darkest hours that we may discover
> the true strength of the brilliant light within ourselves
> that can never, ever, be dimmed."
> Doe Zantamata

How To Be Supportive To Someone Who Is Grieving

When somebody close to you is grieving, remember that it's not your job to "fix" them. It's only your responsibility to provide a good listening ear and allow them to vent about their feelings and how they're handling the loss.

Even though there's only so much you can do to help somebody who's grieving, there are plenty of things that you *can* do to make the whole process a little easier on them. It's all about making them comfortable and providing as much support as possible.

What You Can Do To Help

So, what can you actually do to help somebody who's grieving a recent loss? Here are some of the best things you can do.

- **Be direct.** Don't be afraid to talk about the event, the loss, or how you're feeling about it overall. If your friend or family member wants to talk about it, don't cut them off or try to angle the conversation elsewhere. They might just want somebody to listen to them.

- **Check on them.** You told them to reach out to you if they needed any help, but people in need tend to feel as if they're a burden when they ask for help.

Give a quick call, text, or video chat to ask how they're doing today and what coping has been like.

- **Listen (that's it)!** As much as you might feel like you're good at giving advice, a person who's grieving might just want to vent. They don't want to be told what they *should* do or how they *should* handle it. Just offer a listening ear when they need it most.

- **Be patient.** You might have gotten over a death quicker than your friend, but that doesn't mean they're taking *too* long. Everybody grieves at their own pace, so be patient with them and be supportive (even if you're tired of hearing about it).

- **Offer assistance.** People hate to ask for help, especially if it makes them feel needy. Offer to go to the grocery store for them, cut their lawn over the weekend, or go out to watch a movie they've been wanting to see.

- **Keep them involved.** As much as you might feel like your loved one is delicate right now, that doesn't mean you should leave them out. Even if they say no, they'll appreciate being invited to plans and events that help them to shift their focus somewhere else.

You know your friends and family members best. Just focus on being open to listening and allowing them the right to grieve the loss any way they personally see fit. Unless they specifically ask for advice, leave your opinions and advice to yourself.

When to Suggest Further Help

You love being a source of support for your friend, but it's becoming a little overwhelming. When it feels like it might be a little bit above your paygrade, it's time to suggest professional help. Here's when you should do that.

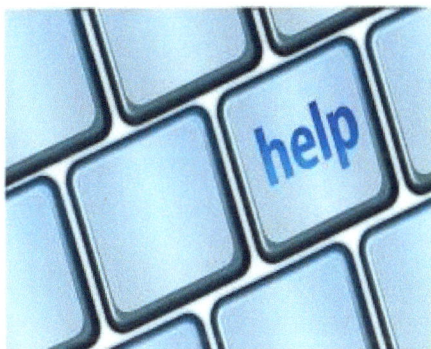

- Any mention of suicide, ending it all, or wishing they were with their deceased loved one

- The grief doesn't come in waves and seems persistent

- They've lost interest in their favorite activities permanently

- They aren't bathing, shaving, cleaning the house, or keeping up with chores as usual

- Their mood is consistently bad, and nothing seems to improve it

Handing your friend's grief over to a professional counselor doesn't mean you weren't a good friend and couldn't do what they needed. Some things are best left to the professionals and it's in your friend's best interest to get professional help.

Above all else, you need to get your friend or loved one immediate help if they've mentioned thoughts or plans of suicide. This is not something that you should be dealing with alone and definitely requires professional intervention.

Final Thoughts

Grief is a process. The good news is that you can heal. You can move forward and live a life that is satisfying, peaceful and fulfilled. The most important thing you can do is keep an eye on your grief and recognize when the loss isn't getting any easier, especially after a lot of time has passed.

Focus on opening up about your feelings and how you're handling the loss. Find yourself a grief group or a grief therapist and develop coping strategies that you can actually implement in your own life.

Keep an eye out on those you love who are grieving. Not everybody likes to show the world that they're in pain, even when they're struggling. If you notice your loved ones struggling through grief, be there for them.

Loss is a part of life but healing from loss is possible. **Stay well and take care.**

"You will survive, and you will find purpose in the chaos. Moving on doesn't mean letting go.
Mary VanHaute

ADDITIONAL RESOURCES

....

SUNDAY GRIEF
7 Steps To Comfort You Through And Beyond Grieving

Have you ever wondered what to do when a family member, close friend, or associate dies? Is it okay to be emotional? Is it okay to have physical or spiritual responses?

Death will occur in everyone's household. Having a road map to transition through the grieving process is priceless. I will share my process through the eye of an Anesthesiologist.

reneesunday.com

NOTE

....

....

....

....

....

....

....

....

....

....

....

....

....

NOTE

....

....

....

....

....

....

....

....

....

....

....

....

....

NOTE

....

....

....

....

....

....

....

....

....

....

....

....

....

NOTE

....

....

....

....

....

....

....

....

....

....

....

....

....

NOTE

....

....

....

....

....

....

....

....

....

....

....

....

....

NOTE

....

....

....

....

....

....

....

....

....

....

....

....

....

NOTE

....

....

....

....

....

....

....

....

....

....

....

....

....

NOTE

....

....

....

....

....

....

....

....

....

....

....

....

....

NOTE

....

....

....

....

....

....

....

....

....

....

....

....

....

NOTE

....

....

....

....

....

....

....

....

....

....

....

....

....

NOTE

....

....

....

....

....

....

....

....

....

....

....

....

....